CLARITY

CREATOR · CREATION · CRISIS · CALLING · CHRIST · CHURCH · CONCLUSION

SIMPLE TRUTH IN A COMPLICATED WORLD

JIM TURRENT

CF4·K

INTRODUCTION

THIS LITTLE BOOK WILL HELP YOU TO LINK TOGETHER THE STORY OF GOD'S LOVE AND TO ANSWER SOME TRICKY QUESTIONS.

We can never understand who God is on our own, and so he has given us his book – the Bible. The focus of the Bible is Jesus Christ[1] who: lived a perfect life – because we can't; died on a cross to take our blame; rose from the dead so that we need not fear death; and who will one day return for all who love and follow him.

Perhaps you have some questions already? *What is God like? How can I know him? Why did Jesus have to die?* Great! We want you to think – and ask questions. That's how we learn.

THE STORY

One of the most exciting things about being a Christian is the discovery that the story of God's love is like a river that flows through history. God spoke to different people at different times, but amazingly, what they wrote down links together and surrounds one person – Jesus Christ! God's book – the Bible – is true and trustworthy. The Bible is God's story and it is given to us so that we may know and trust him. This is why people who love God, love his Word. Why not ask God now to help you understand his message?

---

[1] Jesus means one who saves and Christ means special one.

EACH SECTION OF OUR BOOK IS IN SIX PARTS:

THE BIG THOUGHT: This is the 'big' idea to remember.

BUILD UP YOUR FAITH: Here we look at a part (or parts) of the Bible that will build up our understanding of the Bible. In this part there will be footnotes that might explain something more fully or give you more Bible verses to help you.

BEING CONFIDENT: Sometimes people may tell us that it is silly to believe in God's story that surrounds Jesus, but it's not! In this part we will give you some good answers that will help you.

BIBLE CHALLENGE – MEMORISE THIS VERSE: In this part you will find a verse to memorise. It would be amazing if – by the end of the book – you could remember all the verses!

WHAT WE LEARNED: This is where we recap the main points we have learned.

PRAYER: At the end of each section we will finish by thanking God for what we've learned and then seek to apply it to our lives.

There are lots of things to learn in life, but none are more important than this: that God made you, that he loves you, that he has shown his love in sending Jesus, and that he calls you to follow him. Parts of this book may be challenging, but just as we grow in our understanding of other areas of life, so we must grow in our understanding of God and of the gospel.

So, we think that you're up to this!

Enjoy!

Jim

For answers to questions – see inside back cover

THE CREATOR
THINKING ABOUT GOD

THE CREATOR: THINKING ABOUT GOD

THE BIG THOUGHT

GOD IS EVERLASTING, ONE GOD IN THREE PERSONS

If someone were to ask who you are, you might say something like this, 'My name is Sarah and I was born in Dundee.' When Moses asked God to tell him who he was, God told Moses, 'I am who I am' (Exodus 3). God did not talk about his birth or beginning because God is different from us and doesn't have a beginning. He just is! So, what is God like? God is everlasting, but also an everlasting 'family', Father, Son and Holy Spirit.

BUILD UP YOUR FAITH

God is the creator of all things and has no beginning or end, but what is he like? Perhaps there are famous people like **CELEBRITIES** or sports people that you look up to and enjoy hearing about, but there is no one more amazing to find out about than God. The study of God is called theology and what we discover about God will stretch our minds because – well – **HE IS GOD!**

The Bible teaches us that:

GOD IS ONE

In Deuteronomy 6:4-7 God spoke to his people Israel (we'll talk about Israel later on in the book) and said, 'Hear, O Israel: The Lord our God, the Lord is one. You shall love the Lord your God with all your heart and with all your soul and with all your might. And these words that I command you today shall be on your heart. You shall teach them diligently to your children, and shall talk of them when you sit in your house, and when you walk by the way, and when you lie down, and when you rise.'

> *What are the key words in the above passage? And why do you think that they are key words?*

- *Why does God 'command' us to love him? Why might that not be a strange thing for God to do?*
- *Where do we go to learn about God?*

ONE GOD IN THREE PERSONS

We said earlier that God is different from us in that he has no beginning. But the Bible teaches another amazing thing, that God is one God in three persons: the Father, the Son and the Holy Spirit. Sometimes people try to explain God's three-in-oneness by saying that human beings can be part of one family but remain different people in it – but every explanation like this falls down! The fact that God is one God in three persons is something that only God himself can really understand.

- *Why do you think it's important that God is an everlasting family or community?*
- *What is the word that Christians use to describe God's three-in-oneness? Fill in the missing letters: T R _ _ _ T Y.*
- *Why do you think that some Christians use this symbol to understand God as being one God in three persons? Do you find it helpful?*

Knowing from the Bible that God is one God in three persons, we discover another amazing thing – that God is love. To love, we need an object for our love. Before anything existed – including us – God the Father, Son and Holy Spirit loved each other. This is why we can say that God is love – not just because God loves us – but because he has always existed in love and in kindness, grace, mercy and in all that God is.

BEING CONFIDENT

Someone might ask us: 'Who made God?' God is not like us, he is the uncreated creator and has no beginning. He is not like some ancient gods like Zeus or Thor who 'emerged' (so it was claimed) from the universe. The God of the Bible spoke the universe into being. In our study we also asked 'What is God like?' The answer is that he is one God in a family of three persons. This is why Christians believe that God is everlasting and God is love.

BIBLE CHALLENGE – MEMORISE THIS VERSE

Here is a verse that brings together what we've been thinking about in this study. Psalm 103:17 says **'... the steadfast love of the Lord is from everlasting to everlasting on those who fear him...'**

WHAT WE LEARNED

- God is everlasting.
- God is one God.
- God is one God in three persons; Father, Son and Holy Spirit.
- No one made God – he is the uncreated creator.

PRAYER

GOD – you are amazing. And because you have always been and will always be – your love and promises to us will never end.

Thank you. **AMEN**.

THE CREATION

THINKING ABOUT CREATION

💡 THE BIG THOUGHT

GOD – BY HIS WORD – CREATED ALL THINGS

On the 4th of December 1968, Apollo 8 was orbiting the moon and as it did so, members of the crew read from the first book of the Bible.[2] 'In the beginning, God created the heavens and the earth. The earth was without form and void, and darkness was over the face of the deep. And the Spirit of God was hovering over the face of the waters. And God said, "Let there be light," and there was light' (Genesis 1:1-3). As the astronauts orbited the moon, they saw creation in a new way and their reading of that part of the Bible was just right for those moments. Genesis 1 is clear that God created all that there is and did so by the power of his Word.

👁 BUILD UP YOUR FAITH

God made the world – and indeed everything – so that people would come to know him and to trust him.[3] What is your favourite place in the world? And why? (Apart from your home town/village!) When Paul the apostle went to the city of Athens, he was saddened to see how mixed up the worship of the people there had become. Listen to what Paul said:

"'Men of Athens, I perceive that in every way you are very religious. For as I passed along and observed the objects of your worship, I found also an altar with this inscription, 'To the unknown god.' What therefore you worship as unknown, this I proclaim to you. The God who made the world and everything in it, being Lord of heaven and earth, does not live in temples made by man, nor is he served by human hands, as though he needed anything, since he himself gives to all mankind life and breath and everything. And he made from one man every nation of mankind to live

---

[2] You can watch it here – https://www.youtube.com/watch?v=J_hRRiXKdqc
[3] Read Romans 1:19-20. The Bible says that all people are aware of God.

on all the face of the earth, having determined allotted periods and the boundaries of their dwelling place, that they should seek God, and perhaps feel their way toward him and find him" (Acts 17:22-27).

- *Who do you think Paul is talking about in verse 26?*
- *Why did God make people and give them a place to live? (verses 26-27)*

God has made us male and female and although we are different we are also equal in his sight.[4] The Bible teaches that God made marriage to be between a man and a woman. God has used the picture of marriage as a way to understand the love Jesus has for his 'bride' the church and so God's plan for marriage matters a lot to Christians. There is a lot of confusion about gender today. Whilst we must offer compassion, friendship and help to those who struggle with this, we need to remain lovingly clear that God has made us male and female and that this is good! In all of creation, people are the most special part. This is why Christians – following God's lead – see human life as being very important from its very beginning to its very end. It's great to feel that you're special to your parents or whoever cares for you, but most of all you are precious to God who made you.

Can you think of some really amazing things that people have done?

BEING CONFIDENT

Our universe, our world and everything in it looks very much like it has been designed – that's because it has. It is not at all silly to believe that the design that we find all around us points to a designer. To say there is no God is a statement that cannot be proven. Christians believe that the evidence points us to a creator. If you were walking along a beach and you found your name and address written in the sand, you wouldn't think that

---

[4] Genesis 2:18-25.

this was just the work of the wind or the waves but the work of someone with intelligence. So too, when we find design in nature, it is fair, and not at all foolish, to assume that it points us to the creator and designer of all things.

BIBLE CHALLENGE – MEMORISE THIS VERSE

'The heavens declare the glory of God, and the sky above proclaims his handiwork' (Psalm 19:1).

WHAT WE LEARNED

- God created all things.
- He did this by the power of his Word.
- All people are made by him and for him.
- Design in nature points us to God the designer.

PRAYER

GOD, we thank you that you have made all things by your Word and for your glory. Thank you for sending Jesus so that we might come to know you and worship you as the creator of all things. **AMEN**.

THE CRISIS

WHAT'S GONE WRONG?

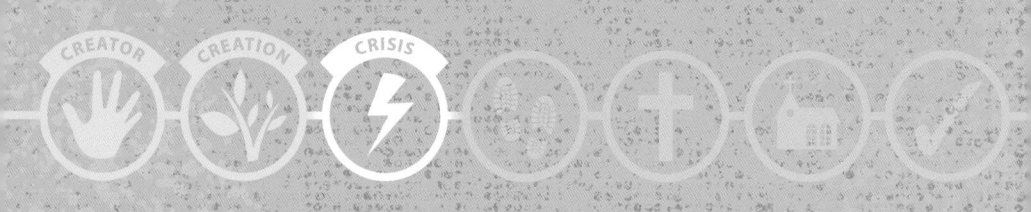

💡 THE BIG THOUGHT
SIN ENTERED IN

Why does bad stuff happen? The short answer is that something has gone wrong with creation – including us. God looked at his creation and declared it to be good – but something happened – and Genesis chapter 3 tells us what that something was. It was the man or woman disobeying God's Word and failing to depend on the God who made them. Because of this a gap opened up between sinful humans and a holy God and creation was affected too.

👁 BUILD UP YOUR FAITH

God had created the man and the woman and placed them in a garden called Eden. In that garden there was lots to eat, but God said that there was one tree that they were not to eat from. This is where we pick up the story as God's enemy, Satan, arrives in the form of a snake:

'Now the serpent was more crafty than any other beast of the field that the Lord God had made. He said to the woman, "Did God actually say, 'You shall not eat of any tree in the garden'?" And the woman said to the serpent, "We may eat of the fruit of the trees in the garden, but God said, 'You shall not eat of the fruit of the tree that is in the midst of the garden, neither shall you touch it, lest you die.'" But the serpent said to the woman, "You will not surely die. For God knows that when you eat of it your eyes will be opened, and you will be like God, knowing good and evil." So when the woman saw that the tree was good for food, and that it was a delight to the eyes, and that the tree was to be desired to make one wise she took of its fruit and ate, and she also gave some to her husband who was with her, and he ate. Then the eyes of both were opened, and they knew that they were naked. And they sewed fig leaves together and made themselves loincloths'" (Genesis 3:1-7).

Now let's trace what happened.

- *Verses 1-3: the serpent causes them to doubt.*
- *Verses 4-5: but this is not where Satan's plan ends for he then gets them to deny God's Word.*
- *The doubt leads to denial and then leads to more sin. They do what God commanded them not to do (verse 3).*
- *And sin is falling short of God's standard. Every one of us has done this that's why we need Jesus (Romans 3:23).*

Because they disobeyed God's Word, the first couple were put out of the garden and were never as close to God again. But God wasn't finished with humans. God promised one to come who would be born like we are but who would conquer our enemy Satan.

- *Can you think who that might be?*
- *How did Jesus defeat Satan?*

The Bible doesn't always tell us what we want to hear, but it tells us what we need to hear. It doesn't tell us that we are okay – but that we need God. Just as Adam and Eve were separated from God when they were put out of the garden, so we are separated from God because of our sin. Help would have to come from God's side. It did. God became one of us. Jesus (God in the flesh) did for us what we could not do for ourselves. He lived a perfect life. He died on the cross to take the punishment for our sin. He rose from the dead because he had won the battle with Satan. Jesus is wonderful. Have you trusted in him?

BEING CONFIDENT

Someone might say to you, 'Are you a Christian?' and you reply 'Sure am!' Then they say, 'Do you believe in talking snakes then?' Cue – much sniggering! What are you going to say? Is your neck going red already? Often the best thing to do is to ask a question back: 'Do you believe that evil is real?' That's a good question – because we have all felt the effects of living in a world gone wrong and this is what Genesis 3 is about. So be confident in God's Word because it is his Word and helps us to understand ourselves, our world and why things are the way they are.

WHAT WE LEARNED

- Something has gone wrong with us and with our world.
- Sin entered the world.
- We must trust God's Word.
- Jesus came over to our side to save us.

BIBLE CHALLENGE – MEMORISE THIS VERSE

God doesn't wait till we're good enough – because we never will be. **'God shows his love for us in that while we were still sinners, Christ died for us'** (Romans 5:8).

PRAYER

DEAR FATHER, thank you for your love for us that reaches deeper than the mistakes we make. **AMEN**.

THE CALLING

CLUES OF THINGS TO COME

THE BIG THOUGHT

GOD CALLS A PEOPLE

All through history, God has been at work calling people into his friendship and making promises (covenants). He made a covenant with a man called Abram[5] (later Abraham), then he made this man's family into a nation and helped them to understand who he is and what his plan will be by giving them his law through Moses. Then follow prophets (like Isaiah) and kings (like David) who point God's people to the future and a king like no other.

BUILD UP YOUR FAITH

ABRAHAM: He was married to Sarai[6] (Sarah) and they couldn't have children. That was sad. But God said to Abraham, 'I will make of you a great nation, and I will bless you and make your name great, so that you will be a blessing. … I will make your offspring as the dust of the earth, so that if one can count the dust of the earth, your offspring also can be counted…' (Why not read the story in Genesis 12–13) What does this tell us about God?

ISRAEL: Later on, Abraham's descendants found themselves in Egypt. They are now called Hebrews, Israelites and later on the people of Israel. After Joseph died, the kings of Egypt treated them harshly. God heard their cries and saved them. When saving them, he told them to do a curious thing. They were to kill a lamb, and put its blood on the doorposts and lintels, God said, 'The blood shall be a sign for you, on the houses where you are. And when I see the blood, I will pass over you, and no plague will befall you to destroy you' (Exodus 12:13).

---

[5] Abram = Father, Abraham = Father of many.
[6] Sarai = Princess, Sarah = Princess of many.

- *Why do you think that blood had to be shed for God to save his people?*
- *Who might the blood be pointing to?*

THE LAW: God gave the law to teach people that he was holy and that they were not and therefore needed him – because they couldn't keep the law. How many of the ten commandments can you remember? (Check out Exodus 20 for the answers.)

PROPHETS AND KINGS: All pointed God's people forward to Jesus. Here are two of them: Isaiah was a prophet and David was a king.

- *Isaiah. Chapter 53 of Isaiah's book is amazing. Take some time and trace every clue of Jesus that you find in that chapter.*
- *David. Peter posed a puzzle at Pentecost. (Try saying that quickly!) Peter asked, 'Why did David call his son 'Lord'? (Lord = God) Do you know the answer? (Acts 2:34-35)*

BEING CONFIDENT

Someone might say, 'All religions are the same so, I won't believe in any!' But all religions aren't the same. Christians have a story that runs through all of history and points to Jesus. This should give us great confidence that this story is not made up. And – just because there are lots of religious 'options' around, it doesn't mean that all of them are equal (when they all say different things) or that one of them cannot be true. Christianity is different because the core truth of it is not about what we do but about what God has done through Jesus Christ calling us and making us his people. It's a story that makes sense. Grace is a great word. Here it means getting what we don't deserve. This is what happens when we trust in Jesus. Now that's different![7]

---

[7] And just because there are different 'kinds' of Christians; Baptists, Presbyterians etc., doesn't disprove anything. There are lots of football teams but they all play football!

THE CALLING: CLUES OF THINGS TO COME

WHAT WE LEARNED

- God calls people to be his people.
- To Abraham – God gave the promise of a people.
- Israel – God saved his people by means of a sacrifice.
- The law – God taught his people what he is like and their need of him.
- Through prophets and kings (and in all of the Bible) God points his people forward to Jesus.

BIBLE CHALLENGE – MEMORISE THIS VERSE

This is God's amazing story: **'Long ago, at many times and in many ways, God spoke to our fathers by the prophets, but in these last days he has spoken to us by his Son'** (Hebrews 1:1-2).

PRAYER

FATHER, thank you for the story of your people in the past and that you are the God whose promises we can trust. **AMEN**.

THE CHRIST

JESUS CHRIST[8] IS GOD IN THE FLESH

[8] Christ means Messiah or God's special and anointed one.

THE BIG THOUGHT

The Lord Jesus Christ is the most significant character in all of human history. In fact – he divides time – BC/AD! The Bible could hardly be clearer about Jesus being both God and human. John 1:1, says of Jesus, 'In the beginning was the Word (Jesus), and the Word was with God, and the Word was God.' Jesus came over to our side to do for us what we could not do for ourselves. He had to be human to represent us and he had to be God to make the rescue possible.[9]

BUILD UP YOUR FAITH

HERE ARE SOME IMPORTANT BIBLE VERSES ABOUT JESUS

1. **JESUS LIVED** 'For we do not have a high priest[10] (Jesus) who is unable to sympathize with our weaknesses, but one who in every respect has been tempted as we are, yet without sin ...' (Hebrews 4:15).

2. **JESUS DIED** 'Christ also suffered once for sins, the righteous for the unrighteous, that he might bring us to God' (1 Peter 3:18).

3. **JESUS ROSE** Romans 1 says, 'He (Jesus) was declared to be the Son of God in power according to the Spirit of holiness by his resurrection from the dead, Jesus Christ our Lord' (verse 4).

4. **JESUS REIGNS** 'After making purification for sins, he sat down at the right hand of the Majesty on high' (Hebrews 1:3).

5. **JESUS WILL RETURN** In Acts 1 as Jesus ascends to heaven the disciples are told, 'Men of Galilee, why do you stand looking into heaven? This Jesus, who was taken up from you into heaven, will come in the same way as you saw him go into heaven' (verse 11).

---

[9] Mark 2:1-12 is a good story that shows the Bible writers thought of Jesus as God.
[10] A priest is someone who represents the people before God.

CRUCIAL CLARITY

Which of the following statements go with which of the above verses?

A *Jesus rules! (Put in the number) (___)*

B *Jesus took the blame and opened the way back to God. (___)*

C *When we trust in Jesus his perfect life is credited to us. (___)*

D *Jesus will return. (___)*

E *This important event showed God's power: that Jesus was no fake; that the Bible is true; and brings hope to us. (___)*

WHY DID JESUS HAVE TO COME INTO THE WORLD?

Because God is holy, this means that he is angry at sin – our sin. Jesus (sent by God) came to help us. He became one of us. Because he is perfectly holy he was able to pay sin's penalty. By his sacrifice on the cross Jesus removed the problem of sin that kept us from God. And there's more… imagine checking your bank account and discovering that someone had transferred in one million pounds! That would be awesome! But the gospel tells us something that is infinitely greater: that when we trust in Jesus he takes our sin and transfers his perfection to us[11] – and God is angry[12] no more.

BEING CONFIDENT

Some might say it's crazy to believe that Jesus is both man and God. But most people who say that sort of thing have never examined Jesus' life. Jesus leaves us no wriggle room when it comes to his claims. He is either mad, bad or who he said he is. The best way to help someone who says that Jesus is not God in the flesh is to ask if they have looked carefully at the source documents. If they haven't – then point them to Mark's Gospel. The Christian faith is evidence based. It is not blind faith but is rooted in

---

[11] Note: this does not mean that we are perfect – because as Christians we will still get some things wrong, but that's how God chooses to see us.

[12] When God is angry he is perfect and angry. But he is also – at the same time – perfectly loving, kind, holy and full of mercy etc.

history and in the testimony of many witnesses. The best explanation of the evidence is that Jesus is both man and God. But do remember that we can't make anyone a Christian. This is the work of the Holy Spirit who takes the Word of God and plants it in people, bringing them alive to God. So pray!

WHAT WE LEARNED

- Jesus is God in the flesh.
- Jesus lived a perfect life.
- Jesus died as a perfect sacrifice in our place.
- Jesus rose from the dead as he and the Bible predicted.
- Jesus now reigns.
- Jesus will one day return.

BIBLE CHALLENGE – MEMORISE THIS VERSE

Grace (here) means receiving something that we have not earned or deserved. This is what happens to us when we become Christians. Paul the apostle put it like this; **'... by grace you have been saved through faith. And this is not your own doing; it is the gift of God, not a result of works, so that no one may boast'** (Ephesians 2:8-9).

PRAYER

HEAVENLY FATHER, we thank you for Jesus and for all he has done for us by his life, death and resurrection. And we thank you for your grace which is giving us what we did not deserve. **AMEN**.

THE CHURCH

WHAT IS IT? WHAT IS IT FOR?

CREATOR · CREATION · CRISIS · CALLING · CHRIST · CHURCH

THE BIG THOUGHT

Have you ever opened a present and wondered what it's for? Awkward! So, what is the church for? The church exists to glorify God by spreading the good news of Jesus and showing the world what a gospel people looks like. The gospel (good news) we speak must be seen in our lives. When Jesus died on the cross he did so, to bring us to God,[13] but also to each other. Being part of a local church is therefore important for us and for the gospel.

BUILD UP YOUR FAITH

Churches aren't perfect – because you and I aren't! Sometimes we can be disappointed with other Christians. But God puts us in the family of the church so that we can learn to forgive (as God has forgiven us) and to follow Jesus as we hear his Word and learn from others about following him. The early church wasn't perfect. The church in Acts 6 had a major problem. But the apostles – and the whole church – left us a great example of how the church should operate. The problem was that some people were not being treated fairly in the distribution of food and so…

'the twelve (apostles) … said, "It is not right that we should give up preaching the word of God to serve tables. Therefore, brothers, pick out from among you seven men of good repute, full of the Spirit and of wisdom, whom we will appoint to this duty. But we will devote ourselves to prayer and to the ministry of the word." And what they said pleased the whole gathering. … And the word of God continued to increase, and the number of the disciples multiplied greatly' (Acts 6:2-7).

- *What was the first thing that we are told the apostles did?*
- *What kind of people did they choose? (verse 3)*

---

[13] This is called the atonement – at-one-ment.

> *What did the apostles see as being very important? (verse 4)*

Three things then happened; unity, amazing growth and generosity as people gave money so that others could be helped.

BAPTISM is Jesus' sign that we belong to him. In the New Testament as people believed in Jesus they were baptised. Baptism is the gospel illustrated. It points us towards the fact that Jesus Christ died, was buried, and rose again. Eternal salvation has been purchased for sinners through Christ's death on the cross. Jesus Christ has defeated the power of sin and the grave. Eternal life belongs to those who trust in Christ and his sacrifice.

What have you learned about baptism that you did not know before?[14]

THE LORD'S SUPPER (or communion) is Jesus' sign of his love for us. The bread reminds us of Jesus' body given for us on the cross where he took the punishment for our sin. The wine is a sign of Jesus' blood[15] – which reminds us of the sacrifice he made. Only those who have first said 'yes' to Jesus and been baptised should eat and drink of the Lord's Supper.[16]

What have you learned about the Lord's Supper that you did not know before?

BEING CONFIDENT

Some people say that they won't believe the gospel because the church is full of people who say one thing and do another! Sadly, sometimes they are correct. None of us are perfect. But part of becoming a Christian involves admitting that we have messed up (and still do) and asking Jesus to forgive us and to help us please him.[17] The good news is that when someone becomes a Christian – they are not only given new life but also the power of the Holy Spirit to live that new life![18]

---

[14] Christians who love Jesus and his Word have different views on who and when someone should be baptised. Ask your parents or church leaders for help while reading the Bible!
[15] Remember the Passover part in the 'Calling' section.
[16] 1 Corinthians 11. [17] This is what we call repentance, which means turning from what is wrong to follow Jesus.
[18] Romans 8 is a great chapter to help us understand this.

WHAT WE LEARNED

- God has chosen to work for his glory through the church.
- The gospel preached *by* the church is to be the gospel seen *in* the church as we love Jesus and each other.
- Baptism is a sign of belonging to Jesus. The Lord's Supper is a reminder of Jesus' love and sacrifice on the cross.
- Being a part of a local church is important.

BIBLE CHALLENGE – MEMORISE THIS VERSE

It's amazing to think that despite our faults God works through the church for his glory in the spread of the gospel. **'Now to him who is able to do far more abundantly than all that we ask or think, according to the power at work within us, to him be glory in the church and in Christ Jesus throughout all generations, forever and ever. Amen'** (Ephesians 3:20-21).

PRAYER

FATHER, thank you for your love for the church and for the privilege that is ours in being part of the greatest movement this world has ever seen. **AMEN**.

THE CONCLUSION

JESUS IS COMING BACK

THE BIG THOUGHT

Jesus promised that he would return. He said this in Acts chapter 1 and in other parts of the New Testament. But like so much of what we learn about Jesus, this teaching of a special day to come was a theme of the Old Testament too.[19] When Jesus returns he will do so as king and judge.

BUILD UP YOUR FAITH

Here are four things that we need to know about Jesus' return.

Jesus will – return in triumph.	'Behold, he is coming with the clouds, and every eye will see him, even those who pierced him ... ' (Revelation 1:7).
Jesus will – raise people from the dead on his return.	'For as in Adam all die, so also in Christ shall all be made alive' (1 Corinthians 15:22).
Jesus will – judge the people of the earth.	' ... he (God) has fixed a day on which he will judge the world in righteousness by a man whom he has appointed; and of this he has given assurance to all by raising him from the dead' (Acts 17:31).
Jesus will – reign in a new creation.	'Then I saw a new heaven and a new earth, for the first heaven and the first earth had passed away, and the sea was no more' (Revelation 21:1).

Is there anything that you have learned so far that you did not know before?

Now look at this passage from 1 Thessalonians 4:13-18:

'But we do not want you to be uninformed, brothers, about those who are asleep, that you may not grieve as others do who have no hope. For since

---
[19] Daniel 7:13-14; Zechariah 14:6.

we believe that Jesus died and rose again, even so, through Jesus, God will bring with him those who have fallen asleep (died). For this we declare to you by a word from the Lord, that we who are alive, who are left until the coming of the Lord, will not precede those who have fallen asleep. For the Lord himself will descend from heaven with a cry of command, with the voice of an archangel, and with the sound of the trumpet of God. And the dead in Christ will rise first. Then we who are alive, who are left, will be caught up together with them in the clouds to meet the Lord in the air, and so we will always be with the Lord. Therefore encourage one another with these words.'

- *Why is Paul (the writer here) so confident that Jesus will return? (verse 14)*

Knowing that Jesus will return brings hope. Jesus' return will be loud (verse 16). News of Jesus' return is given to encourage us (verse 18).

Perhaps you're wondering what happens to people who die before Jesus returns? Someone who dies as a Christian goes immediately into God's presence (2 Corinthians 5:7-9) and awaits Jesus return to earth.[20] Someone who dies rejecting God's message of love is excluded from God's presence forever (Matthew 25:41). It is so important that we know for sure that we believe and follow Jesus; that we tell others about the gospel. We can trust God with those who have already died, because we can be certain that God will always act with perfect justice.

BEING CONFIDENT

Perhaps a friend may say, 'I can't believe in God because of all the suffering in the world.' After listening carefully to your friend[21] you could suggest that if God were to snuff out all the wrong and suffering in the world he would have to snuff us out too! This is because we're part of the problem, we hurt

---
[20] Heaven is the dwelling place of God Matthew 5:16; Revelation 3:12.
[21] Sometimes people may say this because they are hurting inside about something and so it's important that we show our concern for them and listen to them.

one another, tell lies, are part of a world where some have too much and others too little. But God has sent his own Son into our suffering world to die on a cross so that we can be forgiven and follow God's way.

He has also given us the promise that one day Jesus will return, that justice will be done and all injustice will end. This doesn't answer all our questions. But it shows us that God is in control, that he cares, and that we can trust him. What a marvellous message! What a wonderful Lord!

WHAT WE LEARNED

- Jesus will return in triumph as king.
- Those who trust in Jesus now and die will be raised then.
- Jesus will judge the people of the earth.
- Jesus will reign in a new creation that he will bring to pass.

BIBLE CHALLENGE – MEMORISE THIS VERSE

'**Beloved, we are God's children now, and what we will be has not yet appeared; but we know that when he appears we shall be like him, because we shall see him as he is** (1 John 3:2).

PRAYER

OUR FATHER, we thank you that you are in control of all our lives and of history. We thank you for Jesus and the hope of his return. Help us to be faithful so that on that final day we will see him with joy. **AMEN**.

THE END

Wow! That was a lot to take in, wasn't it? We hope that you have learned much that will help you in your walk with God. If there are any questions that you have then feel free to ask your leaders or your pastors. They will be glad to give you an answer or find someone who can!

Here is a summary of the heart of the gospel that might help you.

1. **GOD IS HOLY**[22] – because of this he is angry at sin.[23]

2. **WE ARE NOT HOLY** – but sinful – therefore we have a problem.

3. **GOD SENT A SAVIOUR** – Jesus Christ – so that God's perfect anger would no longer be directed at us.

    - Jesus lived a perfect life. When we trust in him he takes our sin and transfers his perfection to our account.
    - Jesus died on the cross. He did so as a sacrifice to pay sin's debt, and as a substitute to bring us to God.
    - Jesus rose from the dead. This showed that he had conquered death and that God was happy with all that he had done.
    - Jesus sent the Holy Spirit. The Holy Spirit brings us alive to God and gives us the power to live the Christian life.

4. We must therefore trust in Christ and what he has done for us as we receive him as Saviour and Lord of our lives.[24]

When we talk about the gospel, we are not really talking about an idea or a religion – we are talking about a person. When Thomas (the famous doubting disciple) asked Jesus the way to God, Jesus did not say, 'Go this way or go that way' he said, "*I am the way*, and the truth, and the life. No one comes to the Father except through me' (John 14:6). Trust him. Follow him.

---

[22] 'Holy' here means that God is totally perfect.
[23] 'Sin' is an old archery term for missing the mark. Here it means missing God's standards. We are all then 'sinners'.
[24] **1.** Isaiah 6 – **2.** Romans 3:23 – **3.** Romans 3:23; 2 Corinthians 5:21; Acts 2:32,33; **4.** Romans 10:9.